ARCHANGELOLOGY

Michael Protection and Secret Angelic Codes (Archangelology Book Series 2)

ANGELA GRACE

Ascending Vibrations

CONTENTS

Download the 11 + Hour Audiobook 'Angelic Magic v
(Archangelology 7 in 1 Collection)' For FREE!

Get Your *BONUS* Violet Flame Spiritual Cleansing Toolkit vii

Preface ix

Introduction xi

1. MICHAEL THE PROTECTOR 1
   Michael The Person 2
   Archangels and Their Elemental Energies 3

2. HOW TO EASILY CALL UPON ARCHANGEL MICHAEL 6
   Steps for Calling Archangel Michael 7

3. EXERCISES, MANTRAS, AND AFFIRMATIONS 10
   Opening the Mind and Body 11
   Meditation 12

4. PROTECT YOUR LOVED ONES AND PETS 14

5. PROTECT YOUR AURA AND HOME 16

6. ARCHANGEL MICHAEL MEDITATIONS 20

7. ARCHANGEL MICHAEL MANIFESTATION, CHAKRAS, 23
   DREAMS, AND KARMA
   Chakras 23
   Karma 24
   Dreams 24
   Manifestation 25

8. HOW TO TELL WHEN ARCHANGEL MICHAEL IS 28
   AROUND

9. WRITING A LETTER TO MICHAEL 32

10. MICHAEL PROTECTOR REIKI 34

11. DAILY LIFE WITH ARCHANGEL MICHAEL 36

Afterword 39
References 41
Your Feedback is Valued 43

DOWNLOAD THE 11 + HOUR AUDIOBOOK 'ANGELIC MAGIC (ARCHANGELOLOGY 7 IN 1 COLLECTION)' FOR FREE!

If you love listening to audio books on-the-go, I have great news for you: You can download the audio book version of '*Angelic Magic: (Archangelology 7 in 1 Collection - 1. Zadkiel 2. Michael 3. Raphael 4. Metatron 5. Jophiel 6. Uriel 7. Spiritual Discernment)*' for **FREE** just by signing up for a **FREE** 30-day audible trial! See below for more details!

Audible trial benefits

As an audible customer, you'll receive the below benefits with your 30-day free trial:

- A Free audible copy of this book
- After the trial, you will get 1 credit each month to use on any audiobook
- Your credits automatically roll over to the next month if you don't use them
- Choose from over 400,000 titles
- Listen anywhere with the audible app across multiple devices
- Make easy, no hassle exchanges of any audiobook you don't love
- Keep your audiobooks forever, even if you cancel your membership
- And much more.

Go to the links below to get started:
AUDIBLE US : bit.ly/angelicmagic
AUDIBLE UK : bit.ly/angelicmagicuk

GET YOUR *BONUS* VIOLET FLAME SPIRITUAL CLEANSING TOOLKIT

Are you ready to drop all the negative energy that no longer serves you?

- Easily use the violet flame to release blocks holding you back from greatness

- Cleanse your karma to skyrocket your joy
- Start growing spiritually again and get back on the path to your destiny

Violet Flame Spiritual Cleansing Toolkit Includes:

- 1. **Supercharged Energy Clearing EFT Tapping Video:** Download to Banish Negative Energy With the Archangels (Infused with 417 Hz Frequency)
- 2. **Spiritual Cleansing 7 Day Ritual Journal**: Daily Energy Cleansing Ritual Done-For-You; Simply Rinse & Repeat At Home (Print This Out, Stick It On Your Wall, & Cross Off The Days You Complete The Ritual)
- 3. **Powerful 10 Minute 'Spiritual Cleansing With the Archangels' Guided Meditation:** MP3 Download (Infused with 417 Hz Frequency)
- 4. ***BONUS*:** 10 Minute 'Violet Flame' Guided Meditation MP3 Download

Go to: *bit.ly/zadkielmeditation* to Get Your *BONUS* Violet Flame Spiritual Cleansing Toolkit.

PREFACE

This book is for those who often feel vulnerable, unprotected, depressed, anxious, and alone. If you are one of such people, do not lose hope. Saint Michael is filled with light and love, and he wants to dispel these lower energies from your life.

You have not come upon this book or are currently reading this description by accident. This moment has been divinely orchestrated to make you enjoy a fulfilling and happy life on earth.

Those who are already believers in the archangel and divinity in general will find increased enlightenment and a deeper appreciation for the power and beauty of Michael. If you are not a believer, then you are truly fortunate to have found this guide. Michael's energy is ancient, sacred, reliable, and powerful. He can protect you in a crisis and give you courage to face any challenge.

It doesn't take much to invite such supreme and benevolent energy into your life. However, many have failed, repeatedly, to do this. You may even be reading this kind of book (the spiritual kind) for the first time. This guide will reveal to you the simple and effective way to form a lifelong relationship with the archangel.

Each page of this book has been blessed to bring you ever closer to complete healing. From the first chapter, you might feel Michael's warm presence. This, you will learn, is a sign that the archangel is with you. He is on your side.

If you desire the wisdom, protection, and guidance of Archangel Michael, proceed to the first page and be enveloped in light.

This book contains:

- Exercises on mantras and affirmations which you can use to transform the negativity that usually clings to us.
- Archangel Michael meditations and visualizations.
- How to heal your family, friends, and pets with the help of Archangel Michael.
- and much more...

Wishing love and light to all readers...

INTRODUCTION

My life, before I would become engrossed in what one might term esoteric spirituality, was quite lovely. There was nothing particularly striking or fulfilling about it. But with a house that provided a scenic view of the ocean, a relatively rewarding job that allowed for such luxuries, and a spouse who complemented me physically, financially, and mentally, you would agree that a lot of people would envy and aspire for that life. What more could I ask for, right?

To be fair, I *was* grateful for the things and people I had. However, neither material possessions nor a populated and active contact list of mostly superficial friends is enough to give anybody a true sense of fulfilment and success. This is most likely not the first time that you are presented with this school of thought, and you might roll your eyes at it. Yet it stands as one truth that many people would only discover after they have given up years of their life for a false vision of success. I felt divided between trying to be productive at work and being the fun, loveable, and put-together person that my friends and partner expected. This meant that I had very little time (if any at all) to attend to my personal concerns.

Suffice to say that I was constantly enveloped by anxiety, and it wasn't helped by the fact that no one in my life could relate with me. I would reach out to my partner, family members, and friends, but what was now my aching reality seemed abstract for them. As you might expect, this made me think that I must be damaged somehow. I needed some escape. Whenever people are dissatisfied with what they used to long for, they might act out. For me, this was by consuming scary volumes of alcohol and, by any means necessary, demanding a confrontation. Since not many people can exist in the toxic environment I had created around myself, I started to lose those I cared about. My partner called it quits and some of my friends stopped coming back after I pushed them away.

My mental health was in shambles and I was getting increasingly depressed. The combination of a spiraling mental and emotional well-being is never a good recipe for success at work. And, sure enough, my productivity saw an all-time low. The poor maintenance of my body meant that I was constantly ill, and I was quickly coming to the resolve that no longer existing was the only solution to my mess of a life. I no longer had a partner who would miss me. My parents had never thought much of me, and were vocal about how useless they thought I was. My friends, for all I knew, were not only shallow individuals, but they had no emotional connection with me. Taking my own life, at the time, seemed to me a more appealing thought than continued existence.

As you will discover in your journey with the beautiful archangel Michael, nothing in life happens by chance. I would find the light I desperately needed in the most unusual of places—on a shopping trip. I, quite literally, stumbled on crystals in a shopping center. As I moped out of the building while staring at the floor, I bumped into an old lady. This snapped me into reality, and I quickly apologized and bent to pick up her shopping bag. Then I stood up to behold, in a store window, the blue, starry and mesmerizing wonder that was a geode. In my book, *Crystals Made Easy*, I discuss how this moment in time turned me into a fervent crystal collector. Even though I could not explain what made them such spellbinding objects, their beauty and calming effects were irresistible.

Again, fate would direct my path towards further enlightenment and peace. This time, it was through my friend, Linda. All the books I've written, the people I've been able to help, and the joy and contentment that I now enjoy in my life may never have happened without the gentle guidance of the friend who was unlike the others I kept. She came to visit, and we launched into a long conversation about my personal healing, crystals, Reiki, self-acceptance, and more. With her prompting, I continued the research that would bring more concepts like chakras and archangelology into my field of view. I began to let go of the hurt and accepted a peace that was superior to all the mental and emotional trauma I had suffered.

The archangels are superior to every other angel and most supernatural beings. Michael is even more special, as the archangels are his subordinates. He is an especially pretty, yet terror inducing sight. The archangel Michael is often shown in paintings resembling a winged human and wearing colorful robes, exuding light from his face, wings and other parts of his body, and wielding a bright sword. He is God's warrior and the protector of everything pure and good. The first aspect of Michael that I experienced is his ability to heal. As I described earlier, I was broken and felt no reason to continue living. The crystals and Reiki started the healing that I needed, but it was Michael who gave me the determination to continue on that path. Michael has the power to heal the body, mind, and spirit. Through love, he can fill you with the courage you need to dive beyond the hurt and into the depths of your soul where your immeasurable strength and real beauty lies.

I can only imagine that, at this point, you are anxious to know more about this powerful and loving archangel. It is true that the greatest forces in life are those that we cannot see. No one can see depression, yet we feel its grip around our necks and its weight pushing down on our chests. To live without the protection and guidance of Michael is to become overpowered by your fears and hurt. The level of bravery and confidence that you need to stare down a terrifying diagnosis, the loss of a loved one, or extreme loneliness is inhuman. Without confidence and calmness in trying situations, one is most likely to make all the wrong decisions. You need Michael in your life to fight for you and help you stand tall. And Michael does not discriminate. He is willing to help defend even your pets from harm, if you need him to. The mission of this book is to help you see the beauty and necessity of Michael, and teach you the most effective ways to call upon him. I encourage you to open your heart to the friendship of this extraordinary archangel and all the goodness he is prepared to flood your life with.

MICHAEL THE PROTECTOR

Even God must have been in awe of his creation when he named the leader of angels Michael. This name is translated in English as "who is like God?" and the sheer might and courage of this archangel exemplifies this name. In the Bible, we see the loyalty and bravery of Michael at play when he stands up against the rebellion started by Lucifer. With no direct help from the Almighty, Michael battles with the firstborn of the angels and defeats him. The Torah describes an angel who is assigned to be the protector of Yahweh's people, Israel. The Kabbalah, a faction of the Jewish faith, presented the archangel as the one who guides the souls of the righteous into heaven. Muslims also acknowledge the existence and power of Michael. The Quran explains that he blesses the righteous for their good deeds. Michael is able to share his strength of character with those who shun evil and bless them with protection in dangerous situations.

Although the belief in Michael extends to numerous religions, his responsibilities are often the same or similar. Lutherans believe that he is the guardian angel of those whose jobs are inherently dangerous. These include soldiers, police officers, and first responders. Jehovah's Witnesses insist that he and Jesus Christ are the same person. However, the consensus remains that Michael is the loving and magnificent protector of all things good. The Curanderas, who are traditional healers in Latin America, call on Michael to protect everyone from sailors, swordsmiths, the dead and dying, bakers, to bankers. In time of temptation, they ask him for the strength to put up a worthy resistance. The Curanderas create many protective *Amparos* or amulets. One of which is called the Saint Michael Amparo. This particular protective charm is considered one of the strongest, as it is dedicated to the warrior archangel. The Saint Michael Amparo can shield you from lower, malevolent energies.

It is surprising that, as devoted and awe inspiring as Michael is, he is mentioned less than five times in the Bible. Could this be by design? In those few instances where he appears in the Christian scriptures, people attempted to worship him. John in revelations fell to his knees in worship when he was faced with the archangel. This apostle, by all accounts, was fully dedicated to Yahweh and Jesus Christ, and never would have knelt to other gods. But he assumed, through Michael's appearance, that he was in the presence of God. Michael emitted a light so bright that it was impossible to look at him for too long, and his voice could stop the hearts of even the bravest men. As such, he might try to limit his visit to man to avoid being worshipped as God. However, we *can* pray to him, as you will soon learn in this book.

MICHAEL THE PERSON

Note that the word person does not always refer to human beings. In the context of this subtitle, it will be used to describe Michael as a conscious individual who displays emotions, a sense of reason, intelligence, and a complex psychology.

Michael is a fighter, and it is in this role that we often find him in many stories. In his legendary and heroic battle against the devil, Michael single-handedly engages Lucifer in both his angelic and dragon form. Although, there is a lot to learn from this story, it would be remiss of us to ignore the conflict that the archangel Michael must contend with in his existence. You might possess prior knowledge and appreciation for the archangel before reading this book, but you were probably only looking at his status as an icon. If you would like to build a real, loving, and lasting relationship with Michael, then he must have a form outside art and folklore. He must become living, breathing, feeling, and palpable to you. Let's attempt to understand the person that is also Archangel Michael.

He is both a warrior and a healer. You might think that since Michael is the defender of good, it would be easy for him to also be the healer. With appreciation for the complexity of his divine personality, the warrior and the healer are still two distinct archetypes. This is made even more pronounced by the fact that he was created to excel in both abilities.

The warrior archetype puts Michael in a position where he is persistently beset by the need to conquer. Even though he might want to try more peaceful alternatives and appeal to his desire to heal, the archangel cannot afford to be seen as vulnerable. His courage and willingness to keep fighting not only keeps the enemy—Satan, in this case—hesitant, but emboldens the angels in his charge. If all aspects of the warrior archetype stays true for the archangel, then he very likely wrestles his craving for praise and adulation too. Since he is also Michael, the loyal and devoted archangel of God, this can be very challenging when men seem all too eager to bow at his feet.

However, the stories we have heard of Michael and the experiences of those who have accepted him into their lives would suggest that the archangel manages these conflicting archetypes well. He, in fact, seems to favor the healer in him more than the warrior. And when he must defend, we see his loyalty and courage, as opposed to any kind of hubris. as human beings, whether you're a man or woman, we also have the potential to be warriors and healers. And many of us struggle with these choices every day. Since television and popular media would have us think that warriors are violent and that healers often get the short end of the stick, we might respond with aggressiveness when a much calmer frame of mind is a better solution. When you pray and ask for Michael's protection and guidance, it is not wrath or vengefulness that you would feel. Rather, Michael's presence is as energetic as it is peaceful and comforting. We have a lot to learn from the leader of angels, and he is all too eager to teach.

ARCHANGELS AND THEIR ELEMENTAL ENERGIES

Fire

If you have ever seen a painting of Michael, you may recall that he was enrobed in blue cloth or wearing blue armor. At the very least, there is often something blue on his person. This color is symbolic of the might, Godly devotion, and courage that Michael personifies. Other times, the archangel is seen wearing red, which could be a result of his connection to the element of fire. In many religions, fire symbolizes awakening, truth, and purity. Michael can help you pursue not just the truth about your environment, but yourself too. He can hold your hand as you resolve to live a more righteous and disciplined life.

Air

Raphael (which means "God heals") is an archangel who is associated with air. While Michael is both warrior and healer, Raphael's primary role is healer. He can mend every aspect of what constitutes a human being, and help people live more fulfilling lives. He is most commonly depicted in art wearing the color green, which is an energy associated with prosperity and healing. This color also illustrates his connection to the earth. He is quite skilled in making medicines, and can utilize everything from fish to leaves in order to treat injuries and various ailments. Raphael can also help you deal with mental, emotional, and spiritual turmoil. You can call on him for strength, solutions, and guidance if you struggle with depression and addictions. This archangel not only brings new knowledge about general health, but also has a charming sense of humor. If you visit the bookstore and find a healing book on the floor and in your path, this might be Raphael making himself known to you.

Earth

According to science, the earth is about 4.5 billion years old, and life has existed on it for three billion of those years (Redd, 2019). This means that the earth is reliable, and this is a virtue associated with the archangel called Uriel. Another reliable phenomenon is wisdom. Uriel devotes most of his existence to learning and gaining wisdom, and he occasionally shares this with mankind. If you also feel like some parts of your life are out of control, archangel Uriel can grant you stability. His name is translated in English as "God is my light," and he can help you deal with confusion and doubt. As such, students are often encouraged to reach out to Uriel when they are preparing for a test and need the extra support (Patel, 2018).

Water

If you were suddenly asked to name an archangel, Gabriel might be the first that comes to your mind. His name is translated to mean "God is my strength," and you might think that, like Michael, he is frequently in battle. But this is not the case, as God often relies on Gabriel to reveal important information to people. Water is synonymous to clarity and reflection, and

Gabriel's revelations often achieve these two. Typically, his messages are never confusing. Like water, Gabriel helps people to pursue purity of the soul, body, and mind. However, he does not stop at delivering messages. Some of the information that Gabriel conveys can be quite heavy, painful, or even scary to the receiver. This means that the individual would require superhuman strength and courage to take the news and act on it. Gabriel can and does empower people with the boldness to do the will of God and make the best decisions for themselves.

HOW TO EASILY CALL UPON
ARCHANGEL MICHAEL

A s humans, we feel the need to connect, to feel loved, protected, and safe. It's why we marry, have friends, and socialize! But beyond human socialization, there is a part of ourselves that craves a connection to a higher power. One that has driven us to different forms of religions to find answers to our many different questions. In finding answers, we go through different means. But one, which has worked well for me, is calling on Archangel Michael. We've all led pretty long and interesting lives one way or another, but we have also had our down moments as well. Moments when we are at a crossroads, or aren't feeling very good about our current path in life. This point is when you reach out to the archangel, who never fails to show up.

"Why not go to God instead?" you might wonder. The answer is simple: angels are around us every day of our lives, and serve as messengers and servants of the divine. Nevertheless, they aren't gods, and are limited in their abilities and services. The coming of Michael is swift, and you will feel his presence, like a warm light enveloping you with a sense of protection.

Calling upon Michael is as easy as can be. All you need to do is say it or think it. Matter of factly, the mere intention to have him with you invokes his presence. In doing this, you are invoking the divine part of yourself, which is your divine strength, willpower, higher consciousness, and ability to keep yourself space. And as I said earlier, Michael is a part of the divine. Meaning, you are connecting to the same source from which he comes to draw him to yourself. What draws him to you is your willingness and openness to experience his presence.

So, a simple, heartfelt prayer like "I need your help," can invoke the archangel. Think of it as calling a friend. When you pick up your phone and dial a friend for a helping hand, the response he or she would give depends on how urgent help is needed. If there is no urgency, that friend might not show up as quickly as when it's an emergency. But Michael beats any human friend because he shows up regardless of the situation. You need not have an emergency to call Michael. A happy prayer expressing your desire to feel his presence is enough to invoke him.

INTENTION AND WILLPOWER ARE A KEY PART OF CALLING ON ARCHANGEL Michael, because he functions on the ray of divine will. It is that divine consciousness to which you connect to, when you open your heart and mind to call on him. However, when invoking the archangel, refrain from giving yourself away. It's best to not commit yourself to anything not part of you, angel or not. For example, beckoning on him every other time you feel scared isn't advisable, because at those points, you tend to give off the wrong kind of energy. We were all designed as self-sufficient and capable of looking after ourselves. So, surrendering your every fear to the archangel distorts that notion. Also, it means you keep inviting something outside of you to come in and rescue you all the time. If that's not possession, pray, tell, what is it?

Remember that Michael is merely an angel—a guardian of light given to servitude, who doesn't have the willpower to help you without your permission. However, in all your asking, understand that even though he's a part of the divine, you are also a part of that divine wholeness, and are the best protector of your person.

STEPS FOR CALLING ARCHANGEL MICHAEL

1. **Prepare yourself**: There's a reason many appearances of divine beings take place in quiet environments. For one, distractions are less, allowing for divine instructions and interventions without

intrusions of any sort. So, to begin your journey of contacting the archangel, find a quiet spot. To start, concentrate on your breathing and try to relax. Then, imagine yourself surrounded by a brilliant, golden light as you envision the presence of Michael. Allow the energy from within to lift you into the divine realm as you sense the presence of the archangel. With an open heart and a willing mind, reach into your divine self and experience Michael's presence around you. At this point, endeavor to be mindful of everything around you as you wallow in the living and blissful energy he resonates.

2. **Be intentional**: The need for intention cannot be overstated, so be prepared to be granted your needs. The words "I'm ready" is a powerful statement capable of engaging the archangel to fulfil your desires. This statement is especially helpful when you try making positive changes in your life. For instance, if you are grieved, and wish for comfort, you can call on the angel by saying, "Archangel Michael, I'm sad, comfort me. I'm ready to be at peace. Guide me in the divine path towards the peace that I seek. Thank you." Ensure that your needs are positive and not overboard. Remember that the archangel is still limited in what he can do for you. Also, don't spend your time wondering how he will do what you ask. That's not your job. You do the asking, and let the archangel bother with how he's going to supply your needs. Feel free to repeat your needs or intentions again, but avoid nagging. Constantly invoking Michael for the same need shows a lack of faith, which is a bad energy. The divine realm operates with faith, and faithlessness doesn't help. After making your request, listen for guidance or pay attention to any opportunity or ideas that may come your way. It could be Michael offering you intuitive guidance to help achieve your request(s).

As humans, we often require help from others to reach our goals, especially when these goals are related to our life purpose or business. Archangel Michael is a valuable asset to have in such endeavors. Isn't he here to offer divine support and guidance after all? Sometimes, directly asking for help can help with faster replies. Remember, you're an intent away from calling on

Michael and asking him for help. So, don't think about it and just do it. Are you stuck in a situation where you have to think on your feet but have no idea? Say the words. Make a direct request. Michael is at your beck and call, and he will answer in a snap. Do you need the right resources and people to push things forward? He can lead you to them. He's all about guidance after all, isn't he? He will whisper your name to those people that matter, and they will contact you.

1. **Visualize help coming**: Picture Archangel Michael attending to your needs and rounding up other angels to help you. Envision a golden light bathing you from heaven as you receive that idea, opportunity, or contact you asked for. Don't worry. Don't fret. Don't doubt. Just open your mind to the possibility of your request being answered. Feel your energy grow as you absorb the divine intervention of Michael. Believe that the situation is in control, and that the archangel is doing as asked to get things running. If you feel your request is taking too long to be processed, or help doesn't come as quickly as you like, don't be discouraged! It could be a test of faith to validate your trust in the divine power. Losing your faith would mean that you never truly believed in the ability of the archangel to bring your wishes to life. Hold fast to your faith and wait for the answers, which will come in their due time.

3

EXERCISES, MANTRAS, AND AFFIRMATIONS

T he Indians believe in chakras, the Chinese chi; but one thing remains common regardless of beliefs: we are all made of energy. The universe is a vast span of expanding energy in various degrees, and we are a part of this energy. In moments when we are down, sad, or unexcited, we experience a period of low energy. In contrast, when we are at our highest and happy, we radiate positive, vibrant energy. These energies are what help us stay grounded and connected to the universe and those around us. Without them, we would be incapable of connecting with the divine. Think of the divine as a sacred energy channel, like a plug you connect to for the surge of the supernatural. When you connect your phone to an outlet using a charger, the battery receives a surge of energy that powers it. That is exactly how our connection to the divine works.

According to Buddha, living is suffering, and he couldn't have been more correct. We live life trying to survive and do better than we did the previous day. Put simply, we are on a merry-go-round of avoiding suffering. Meaning, we are constantly surrounded by negative energies that may disrupt the brilliance of our intrinsic energy. This explains why we need to engage the archangel, Michael, to help drive any form of negativity that might cling to us. But such a feat cannot be achieved by wishful thinking or speaking the word. For instance, to improve your battery percentage, you have to plug in your phone. So, to get rid of negative energy, you have to plug into the energy channel. Let's consider another instance: when tragedy strikes, we tend to send thoughts and prayers or love and light to those in distress. It doesn't seem like much, but in doing that, we tap into their energy, putting ourselves in their shoes. In turn, we give them some positive energy to help them through the dismal situation. There are no benefits to taking on the pain of others, and you must understand how these energies affect you.

The divine isn't a physical channel you can plug into; thus, begging the question: how do you connect to it? There are several exercises, mantras, and affirmations that can get you hooked, but they all boil down to the technique of opening your mind and body, and aligning your energy. An open mind is one that perceives, and an open body is one that receives! In opening your mind, you create a means of connection with the archangel, and an open body presents a route through which positive energy is received.

OPENING THE MIND AND BODY

Exercises to Open the Body

1. Find a quiet place to sit. Ensure that the place is comfortable, so you don't get distracted by discomfort over time.
2. Sit upright with your spine aligned, and your chest pushed forward slightly in a receiving position. This posture opens up the body to receive the energy. Aligning the spine allows the energy channels within you to connect throughout the body, from your crown to the base of your spine.
3. You can hold up your hand in a prayer-like posture, but this is optional.
4. Close your eyes to shut out distractions from the environment. Doing this will allow you to be more aware of what is going on within you.
5. Be in tune with your body, and block out your perception of the external environment.
6. Listen to your breathing, and focus on it until you feel yourself grow calm with each breath.

Exercises to Open the Mind

1. The first step is to be mentally prepared for the process. Be intentional about wanting to receive positive energy and dispel negative ones.
2. Clear your mind. Avoid thinking about anything at this point. It can be challenging, given how the mind can be easily distracted! But focus on nothing more than the goal, which is to connect to Michael.
3. As you picture the archangel, take in deep breaths through your nostrils. Visualize the breaths you draw as living, positive energy.
4. Hold your breath for about seven seconds before exhaling through your mouth. Picture the exhaled breath as negative energy leaving your body.
5. Repeat the breathing exercise for as many times as you feel necessary.
6. On your final exhalation, picture the positive energy you have taken in flooding your body with light. Picture it revitalizing you, charging your mind and body.

MEDITATION

The technique of opening your mind and body leads up to the final technique, which combines mantras and affirmations to rid you of those pesky negative energies. While meditating with the archangel, he will protect and shield you from negative energies, helping you rise to the strongest version of yourself!

As you imagine your body being recharged by the healing power of the positive energy you inhaled, you can use this mantra (or other affirmations) to call on Archangel Michael:

"Now, I call in all my guides to be present with me, including all those that are in the highest of love and light: Archangel Michael, guardians, spirit guides, ascended masters, and loved ones. I ask that you surround me with your healing light, and rid me of my attachments to negative energies like worry, stress, and any other lower energies. Help me to be free from any attachment to fear. Help me to let go of my ego, as I ascend into the higher place of my being that only sees and knows love.

I ask that you take away any old energy still within me, and retract any form of thought that takes semblance to fear and ego. Help me to reconnect with the fragments of my soul, experiencing the wholeness of my divine birthright. And as I let go of every form of stress and fear, may I feel the intrinsic divine power at work in me. That I may be filled with the courage and strength to know my identity and work in the divine light. As I breathe in and out, I refill and recalibrate my mind and body with the divine energy that bursts with love, joy, and peace. I ask, Archangel Michael, that you shield me, sealing these positive and whole vibrations into my physical and emotional bodies.

I ask that you stay with me, helping me to continue in the divine light of God. Amen."

4

PROTECT YOUR LOVED ONES
AND PETS

Loved ones are more than a set of people who share the same surname with you. They are the people who rejoice, mourn, and stay by your side throughout the rest of your life. They are the ones you call home, without whom there would be no memories to make or cherish or recall. They are family that back you and friends that cheer for you. The ones who are there when you hit a roadblock. The people you call when in need. They are everything that makes life meaningful. As such, they must be protected. You can call on Michael to protect your loved ones, and keep them safe. You can pray for their protection and happiness in the same way you pray for yours.

Like family, pets are the perfect balance of happiness and anger. We love when they snuggle close to us when we sleep, but are horrified when they take a leak on the car seat. So, basically, they are family. Due to how much time we spend with our pets, we tend to develop strong bonds with them. To the extent that they sometimes put themselves on the line to save their human friends. With this in mind, it makes sense why you should not leave your pets out of your prayers. These animals are a source of joy, love, compassion, and peace to us, especially when we are at our lowest moments.

Committing your pets into the protection of Archangel Michael makes them safe and sound even in your absence. While it might sound silly to invoke the archangel around your pet, it is no strange tradition. In Christendom, animals played a crucial role in the liberation of the Israelites. More so, they were one of God's earliest creations, and our relationship with them stretches as far back as Noah and Adam. Pets have a more limited lifespan than us humans, meaning we will most likely witness their passing at some point. This can be a low point in our lives, so we have to make the most of the time we have with them. To ensure that they live out their days, you have to commit them into the care of Archangel Michael.

Remember the story of the Passover? When the Israelites smeared the blood of an animal on doors of their houses and the Angel of death spared them? The Archangel is not beyond catering to our pets and loved ones if we ask him to protect them. He is a guardian and a servant of light, so he is obliged to help you. And since they are family, he is obliged to protect them as well. Call upon the Archangel as you would at any time by reaching into your inner connection with the divine. Bid him to come to you with his host of guardian angels, and ask him to surround your loved ones and pets. Ask him to protect them from the evil of the days and the pestilence of nighttime.

Here is a prayer you can use:

"Dear, Archangel Michael, I ask that you come to me with your host of angels." As you say this, visualize him descending to meet you with his band of angels in a brilliant blue light. "I ask that you surround my pets and loved ones (family and friends), and shield them even as you shield me." You can call the names of your loved ones and pets. "Protect them from negative energies and the results of their errors. Give them your guidance to walk in the divine light, that their paths may be illuminated by the brilliance of your divine light. Be by them all day, every day. Be their guide and defender. Amen."

Now, visualize Archangel Michael dispatching his angels to surround your loved ones and pets. They are safe now, thanks to you!

5

PROTECT YOUR AURA AND HOME

I n our day-to-day lives, we experience negative vibes around us, coming in the form of colleagues, family, friends, social media, and even the mass media (who especially thrive on reporting gloomy news). Even the people you find on the streets, at the marketplace, and any other public place tend to have a low energy about them. Public places aren't usually cleansed or protected, and with people going about with low energies, it's easy for you to pick it up. The longer you stay exposed to these low energies, the higher your chances of noticing the effect of those negative vibes. This explains the importance of cleansing both your body and environment, as they work hand in hand to define your energy levels and aura.

Asides experiencing low energies from the physical world around us, we also have to be wary of negative vibes that can be picked up from the spiritual realm. But don't beat yourself up about this detail, because you have a shield in Archangel Michael, who will be there to guard and warn you at all times. All you have to do is ask. However, bear in mind that you can unintentionally let in energies that won't act in your best interests. For instance, following a depressing situation due to curiosity can introduce negative energies into your aura. But with the right form of protection from Archangel Michael, and the intention and willingness to connect with your spirit guides, you will be able to avoid crossing paths with the wrong energies.

But how would you know you haven't picked up any negative vibes or low energy if you can't see them? It's easy to find out if you have low energy or negative vibes, because you will experience crankiness and exhaustion. So, even after a good night's rest, you would still wake up feeling drained. You may especially feel this exhaustion at noon as you constantly try to avoid dozing off. As this continues, your focus will be diverted, and it becomes a chore to go through your daily tasks. However, it could also be that you feel ill, because poor health can also be responsible for exhaustion and low energy. As such, do well to see a doctor first to confirm you are in good health. However, if after trying everything, and you can't find any underlying health concerns, then it's time to focus on the spiritual part, which is cleansing your energy to rid yourself of low or negative energy.

Alternatively, to ensure that you get it right and remove every form of low energy safely and entirely, you can try seeing a therapist, but not just any therapist will fly with this task! You need an expert at removing low or negative energies and cleaning auras. Ensure to take the time out to carefully select the right therapist for the job. He or she has to be able to carry out the procedure safely, so they don't damage your aura any further or let in more negative energy. If you can't find a therapist to help with this, you can do it yourself. All you need is the archangel Michael to get rid of those low energies within and around you. Steps on how to carry out the procedure yourself will be covered in a later part of this chapter.

How can you use Archangel Michael to protect and cleanse your energy and aura?

We have all been in the position when someone needed help. At that point, you have a choice to let the energy of others affect yours. For instance, someone may have asked you to attend to their needs and forego whatever you were doing at some point. You ended up saying yes, even though you really wanted to say no. Or, have you helped someone out only to return feeling drained for days, and can't understand why? Then you get a text from the person you helped telling you how good your help was to them, and how they feel great. This happens because you swapped your positive energy for their negative one. So, you take home their burden, and leave them with your wholeness. Here is a step by step guide to rid your aura and environment of negative energy:

1. Every morning, visit your quiet place. Start by grounding yourself with some breathing exercises to calm your mind and body and reduce distractions. Shut your eyes, and listen to your breathing until you block out every sound from your physical environment.

2. Next, invoke the archangel Michael using a mantra of your choice. You can use: "Archangel Michael, I invite you to this place right now. Let me feel your presence." Now, envision him coming to you, and ask for protection. "I ask you to protect me as I commune with you. Guide my heart and mind, and shield me from distractions." Practice your mantra regularly until you know it by heart. Knowing it will help you summon Michael faster.

3. As you meditate, prepare your mind and heart to draw the archangel to yourself. Take a deep breath, and feel the radiation of his angelic energy surrounding you. You may see the blue energy he radiates, or feel it around you.

4. Picture yourself as an airship surrounded by Michael's divine blue light. Imagine other airships taking shots at you with several weapons. These weapons are the negative energies being sent your way. Envision these attacks bouncing off Michael's light, as you stay safe within the shield of his presence. Practice this when you run into someone radiating negative energy, or listen to some negative happening on the news. Picture yourself shielded by Michael, so that the negative energy has no effect on you. Doing this means you are reinforcing your intention to be under Michael's protection. Then, mutter to yourself or think about Archangel Michael standing next to you with his host of angels. Imagine them fending off the negative energy, and preserving your positive energy. Doing this doesn't mean you are less interested in helping others. No, you can help others as much as you want. Just ensure to do it safely within the confines of Michael's protection to protect yourself from swapping energies. As a matter of fact, you are in a better position to help others when you take care to cater for your energy.

5. After fortifying yourself against negative energies, the next step is to extend that protection to your environment. From your car, to your work area, to your house, to every other place you spend

time at. To fortify these places under Archangel Michael, all you have to do is envision his light spreading from you around your present environment at any one time. Picture that place bathed in that brilliant blue light that surrounds you.

6. Remember, the archangel Michael can be reached at any time. The construct of day and night doesn't apply to him, so he is ready to protect and shield you at any time. All you have to do is say the word, and he will be obliged to help you. Also, you can extend this protection to the places of your loved ones too.

⚜ 6 ⚜
ARCHANGEL MICHAEL
MEDITATIONS

editation is a process that combines several techniques such as concentration and mindfulness to achieve a certain goal. When meditating, you focus on a specific activity, thought, or object and train your awareness and attention on it until a clear, stable, and calm emotional and mental state is reached. In this chapter, the objective of this meditation is to call upon Archangel Michael and bask in the comfort of his protection.

A step-by-step guide on how to call upon the protection of Archangel Michael is covered below:

1. Shut your eyes and relax your body. Soften yourself and let go of any tension.
2. Focus on your breathing: inhaling and exhaling. Breathe deeply and let go of anything that doesn't serve you in the here and now. Release them as you exhale.
3. Train your focus on the present moment, and take note of your breathing.
4. Prepare your mind with the intention to feel supported, protected, and safe.

5. As you take deep breaths, feel your consciousness sink deeper, traveling further into yourself as you anchor onto your soul space.

6. From this space, call on Archangel Michael to come to your aid. Invite him from the divine realm to be present with you now.

7. You might experience him in a human-like or angelic form, or as the blue energy he radiates.

8. As he presents himself to you, you will feel every anxiety, worry, and stress melt away.

9. In the presence of the archangel Michael, you can only feel protected, loved, and safe.

10. As we've talked about throughout this book, you are created with free will. So, the only way the archangel can step in to help you is if you ask. So, ask him. "Please, Archangel Michael, keep me safe. I ask that you keep this feeling of security and safety with me always. Please, protect me wherever I go."

11. Envision the archangel receiving your request and casting a ball of blue energy around you as a protective sphere to protect your energy from being depleted or disrupted by any external force, so that your energy might be protected from those that will drain you, or anyone that wants to take from you what you aren't willing to give up.

12. Take a deep breath in this space filled with love, protection, and safety. Enjoy the feeling of knowing that within the confines of this space, you can't be touched by anything that can affect you negatively.

13. Know that Archangel Michael is by your side all the time, willing and ready to come forward and help you find your way to this space whenever you feel like reconnecting. All you have to do is ask.

14. Thank the archangel for his presence and the divine blessings he has showered you with.

15. Commit to take this feeling of protection, love, and safety with you as you return your consciousness to your physical body.

16. Breathe in deeply as you ground and anchor yourself to this blissful feeling.

17. Slowly, make some gentle movements like stretching and opening

your eyes when you feel ready to return back to your day.
Remember to reconnect to your protective sphere whenever you
feel negative energy or emotions.

The benefits of this meditation routine cannot be overstated. Not only does it allow you to take charge of your day, it also helps you start out and finish on a high note. This spells a great frame of mind for you, which would allow you to function at the top of your game throughout the day! Also, with that much positive energy, you will be able to help others and spread the good vibes.

⚝ 7 ⚝

ARCHANGEL MICHAEL
MANIFESTATION, CHAKRAS,
DREAMS, AND KARMA

CHAKRAS

Chakras are energy centers or inner lights within the body that are lit up when we meditate. In Eastern religions, they are usually depicted as spinning wheels. A smooth and fast spin shows a higher likelihood of connecting with the divine. The idea behind this notion is that angels can be summoned through meditation and their respective connections to the chakras in the body. When chakras spin, they produce unique divine vibrations that connect to the divine realm. Angels respond to their chakras and grant us our requests. Sometimes, chakras can also be a source of connection for angels who wish to communicate with us. This is especially so for chakras like the solar plexus, heart, and crown chakras, from which we received intuitive guidance.

Archangel Michael is responsible for the throat chakra. So, when you connect with him, you are tapping into and activating the throat chakra. This chakra is linked to the color blue, hence Michael's distinct aura. Blue gems like sapphires can help you connect with the throat chakra and Archangel Michael better. But sometimes, the chakras can get blocked, cutting off your connection with the divine. To prevent this, here is a prayer to help you cleanse your chakras system:

"Archangel Michael, please come to me. I ask that you purify and cleanse my entire chakric system. I ask for your pure, concentrated light to flow through me, cleansing, purifying, and strengthening my chakras. Let the energy within me grow under your guidance, fueling my chakras with your love and blessings. Let every bad energy within me, blocking my chakras be completely erased now and forever. Amen."

KARMA

Karma is a relatively common term, which is feared by many. While karma should not be feared, it should absolutely be respected! Karma is usually drawn by your actions. As much as you have free will to do as you please, you also pass judgement on yourself for your deeds. Karma is believed to be accrued from previous lifetimes. According to the belief, you decide what is missing in your life and how to go about it. The next time you reincarnate in a different lifetime, the choice is yours to choose what you have to learn. It's at this point that karma steps in. For instance, if you hurt someone in a previous lifetime, you will pay for that hurt if you don't unlearn the toxic behavior.

DREAMS

Archangel Michael works with us when we dream to help ease our fears, and guide us to new peaks of peace and happiness. He teaches us when we sleep, and provides answers to our questions. He helps to construct the foundations of our purpose in life as we lay lost in slumber. Even though you don't remember your dreams sometimes, the information they contain isn't lost to your subconscious and aids you in several ways. To access the counsel Michael offers during sleep, you can keep a dream journal to record your dreams. You can use any notebook. Ensure to keep said book close to you as you go to bed, so you can easily record your dreams. Over time, you will start to see patterns in symbolisms and themes that will guide you when you wake.

When you have recurring dreams, it's likely that Archangel Michael is emphasizing on a particular subject, so pay attention. Get a book on dreams or reach out to a dream expert if you are confused or need guidance. Also, ensure to get a good night's rest. Refrain from retiring to bed intoxicated because chemicals tend to disrupt dream sleep (REM sleep). Here is a prayer to call on Archangel Michael before bed:

"Archangel Michael, I thank you for putting me to bed and helping me to enjoy sound sleep. I ask that you come into my dreams to teach, heal, and guide me. I beg that you show me (mention any request about a situation) on a spiritual level. Guide me to your understanding. Amen."

MANIFESTATION

The world we live in thrives of experiences and variety. Every one of us has the inherent ability to give life to what we desire the most.

Manifestation is a natural occurrence that happens regularly for as long as we live, and is independent of whether or not we are aware of it. You can begin living in dominion, feel empowered, and have your needs met when you own your ability to manifest whatever you choose. We are blessed with the ability to merge with the divine in conscious co-creation. This ability is one that can be harnessed through a variety of ways, particularly through Archangel Michael. In this chapter, we will explore some of the most powerful and consistent methods of reaching for and focusing on the power of manifestation deep within us. To tap into this ability, one key element is intention. Unconsciously, we spend our days setting intentions as we go, in conversations, our mind chatters, and even to-do lists. These three examples are some of the basic forms of intentions we set.

However, the magic doesn't come from setting intentions unconsciously, but when we become mindful of the process and align it with our energy and perspective. It's all about posing yourself and being deliberate about receiving and giving. One of the most potent ways to create intentions is with a specific ritual, like the meditation we covered in the previous chapter. That said, intentions need certain elements to function, some of which includes:

- being conscious and deliberate
- maintaining integrity and authenticity in your demands
- trusting your intentions

- keeping a flexible and clear mind
- staying emotionally prepared

How to call on Archangel Michael for manifestation, positive shifts, and imaginative power.

1. **Be clear about your goals:** To manifest your desires (wealth, power, dominion, etcetera), you must know what you want. Otherwise, you can't take any steps to make it work, and summoning the archangel would be in vain!

2. **Ask Archangel Michael:** Once you know what you want and align your intentions to it, the time is right to tap into your innermost self, connect with the divine, and invoke the archangel. Tell the archangel what you want to manifest for him to begin the process.

3. **Work towards achieving our results:** Remember, manifestation is the process of co-creating the divine. So, working towards reaching your desires improves the likelihood of getting what you want. For instance, if you wish to manifest wealth, don't stay idle. Get busy!

4. **Believe in the process:** As you commit to work towards your desires, you might tend to doubt the feasibility of manifestation. Frustration and discouragement is only natural. Don't sit in the struggle, pondering what went wrong, or if things could work out. Doing that means you don't trust Archangel Michael enough to come through. If you are too afraid to fly for fear of a crash, you will never know what it feels like to be above the clouds.

5. **Be open to receiving and acknowledging what you get:** Archangel Michael is present to give you help along the way as long as you ask. However, it's easy to miss his signs, especially when they don't come in the way you expect. The minute you begin acknowledging and receiving the signs given by Archangel Michael, you will succeed in whatever you do.

6. **Maintain high spirits:** Based on the universal law of attraction, you get what you give. A classic case of what goes around comes

around. If you want to get more of what you want, commit to walking with Archangel Michael and adhering to his guidance.

7. **Check for resistance:** Sometimes, it's not that Archangel Michael hasn't granted your wishes, it's that you might be resisting it. Resistance comes in the form of frustration, fears, doubts, procrastination, among other negative emotions. Keep a clear head, and ask for his guidance in removing these resistances.

HOW TO TELL WHEN ARCHANGEL MICHAEL IS AROUND

Life is never one smooth and happy ride until our passing, unfortunately. At many different points, we will be faced with difficult choices, uncertainty, fear, grief, and other challenging situations. Sometimes, the shoulder of a loved one is enough to keep us from falling. But, more often than not, we need our spiritual guides. In many trying moments, nothing else will do except, quite literally, the help of an angel. Thankfully, angels know when we are in trouble and the precise help to offer. They are everywhere, and might be beside you as you read this book. They, however, refrain from tinkering with human choices and its outcomes without permission. They might get involved to stop evil occurrences in times when people may not have the chance to say a quick prayer and invite the help of angels—as in the case of car crashes and the likes. In most cases, they stand aside and try to make their presence known in several ways.

The archangel Michael, can be especially persistent when trying to communicate his presence. Those who are ignorant of the operations of spiritual entities may just chuck it up to gut feelings. However, those who have taken the time to gain knowledge on this subject are comforted by the signs that are outlined below.

1. **You feel at peace:** Although this sign is common to all the

angels, Michael's peace is more comforting than most. He often appears in crisis situations, when human judgement is ordinarily impaired. It is, in fact, in such scenarios that we notice his unmistakable calm the most. You can also feel the peace of the archangel when you are anxious and angry. He envelops us in his wings and will stay for as long as we need him to.

2. **You see his aura:** In chapter 1, we saw that archangels are associated with certain colors. These colors are their auras, and every angel has one. It glows brilliantly, and might be observable by humans in some cases. Michael's aura is blue. If you suddenly see a shimmer or flash of blue, this could be the archangel making himself known.

3. **You come upon a feather:** As pointed out earlier, Michael is a very persistent angel. He understands that human beings are doubtful creatures and that we are not likely to be convinced by one sign. As such, he will leave multiple clues to help you recognize his presence. One of such clues is a feather. If you remain skeptical after seeing the light of Saint Michael's aura and feeling the angelic calm, you might begin to see physical evidence of the fact that he is close to you. This is a calling card that should awaken and reassure you of God's love. It should neither alarm, nor scare you in any way.

4. **You hear his voice:** Have you ever been upset or anxious about any matter, and then you hear, seemingly out of nowhere, someone speak? This might be in a whisper or a more audible tone. If the voice seems to come from no apparent source, this could be an angel trying to communicate with you. Michael might whisper to you or speak in his characteristic clear, deep voice. While hearing his voice might be a bit jolting, his words and messages are those of peace and love. Oftentimes, they are also laced with humor. He wouldn't be forceful or commanding. Remember that Saint Michael is also a healer, and he is gentle with humans.

5. **You see his name everywhere:** How often do you hear or see the name Michael in a day? Even if you have a friend, pet, and sibling named Michael, and you live on Michael street, chances

are that you won't stumble on the name at every turn or hear it at work, in your car, and other places that aren't your street. So, if this happens, don't be quick to dismiss the sign. This is even more true when you find the name three times. You might receive help from someone named Michael (or Michelle) or hear the name on the radio. It is more rewarding for you to acknowledge the archangel's presence, accept his heavenly calm, and ask for his help where you need it.

6. **You know it's the truth:** "Am I just hearing what I want to hear?" you might ask yourself. However, Michael's signs and messages cannot easily be dismissed as an overactive imagination. Whether they are practical or easy, it will be clear that you are neither hearing a lie, nor seeing an illusion. While the ego is powerful and cunning, it is incapable of mimicking angelic signs and messages.

7. **You feel hot:** You might feel a warm sensation when Michael is close to you. Before adjusting the air conditioner or worrying that you might be coming down with something, consider the possibility that an archangel has honored you with his presence. This warm feeling is noticeable even in generally cold temperatures. Michael, as we saw in chapter, is associated with fire. This is not just an element that is imagined by artistes and storytellers. It is a truth. Michael is often regarded as a sun deity by some because of the sheer amount of heat that he conducts. Thankfully, Michael will not cause you any harm with this heat. It often feels no hotter than the rays of the sun on a warm afternoon.

8. **You see repeating numbers:** Again, how often do you see the number 777? Even accountants and mathematicians rarely stumble on a specific order of numbers multiple times in a day. Since we always expect randomness in many aspects of our daily experience, Michael could try and get your attention with some order and repetition. You may have heard a lot about 11:11 and now reflexively dismiss such phenomena. However, the fact that you are now reading this book means that you want to be more open-minded to the idea. You have everything to gain by doing so.

When next you find repeating numbers throughout your day, know that Saint Michael is reaching out to you.

9. **You see symbols of protection:** This usually happens after someone prays to Saint Michael. Think of what makes you scared, anxious, or apprehensive. When you call to the archangels in such times, he immediately wants to help. To do so, he might direct your attention to objects that symbolize his protection over you. He will also provide you with the clarity to understand the meaning of such symbols. You might see a cross while waiting to be called for an interview. If you feel anxious about going out in public, you might notice a sword—this could be as a mural or on a poster. Even umbrellas can be shown to you by Michael, since they provide a hiding place from the rain.

10. **You hear his guidance as your thoughts:** In the depths of a depression, it is nearly impossible to have uplifting or optimistic thoughts. If you have ever gotten to such a point in your life, then you fully understand the ever-sinking feeling that follows depression. Even worse is the fact that you might want to keep drowning in the negativity and darkness that cloaks your mind. If you ask Michael for help, your mental image of your situation will gradually become less bleak. First, you will feel calm and relaxed. You might have a funny thought and chuckle. Then you gain an astronaut's perspective of your life, and all your problems will become less overwhelming than they were. This is Archangel Michael speaking to you through your thoughts.

❧ 9 ❧

WRITING A LETTER TO MICHAEL

W hen you love and trust someone, you would miss them when they are not around. In the case of your relationship with the archangel, that would be when you *feel* they are not around. You enjoy communicating with them as often as possible, and employ various means to do so. Thankfully, Michael is ever ready to listen, reply, and assist you. You can communicate with him meditatively through prayer, and by writing letters. Not everyone is experienced with being still and meditating. Also, you might have doubts about your prayers reaching Michael (you shouldn't), and want something physical to strengthen your belief.

Before writing the letter, it is important that you *know* that you are worthy of angelic attention! These powerful spiritual beings have loved you unconditionally from the moment your soul was created by God. They never want to lose sight of you, and are eager to help you. Uncertainty and self-doubt might affect your expectation, which could hinder you from hearing your angel. Cynicism and dishonesty may also hinder your communication with Michael. You must be sincere when writing to him!

While writing the letter, do not be surprised if you feel the presence of the angel you are trying to reach. For Michael, as you already know from the previous chapter, this is the warm sensation, comforting feeling, and glowing, blue aura. As you pour your heart out in your letter, the archangel's presence might become more palpable. This is him urging you to hold nothing back. Express the full range of your emotions—from hurt feelings to gratitude— and make all your requests known. You can ask Michael to grant you physical or emotional healing. If you need the help of a therapist, ask him to guide you to the right one. Ask for courage and his protection if you are about to engage in something that is both positive and dangerous. Archangel Michael can also ensure that you get justice when you deserve it. But your requests do not necessarily have to be serious. You can ask for Saint Michael's help to fix a faulty television set. At the end of this exercise, you might choose to burn the letter or save it, but be confident in your belief that you have been heard.

Arrange the letter like you would if you were addressing a close friend. Write the angel's name at the top of the page, and follow this with your name and the date. Now, write *Dear Archangel Michael*, and begin expressing your sincere thoughts. You can sign the letter by writing thank you, yours faithfully, I love you, or whichever way feels right to you. That's it. Your letter has been sent to and received by Michael.

The archangel might reply through your dreams. As such, it is important that you do not sleep late or wait until you are exhausted before going to bed that night. You want to be able to remember what instructions and revelations are shown to you. When you wake up, record what you saw while dreaming. This can be done by writing down what you remember or using a video or audio recorder.

❧ 10 ❧

MICHAEL PROTECTOR REIKI

The modern-day practice of Reiki is credited to the 20th century Japanese monk, Mikao Usui. He taught his students, as he believed, about the various energies that traveled through the human body, and how these could be guided to help people achieve a more relaxed and happy state of being. Mikao Usui would place his hands a few inches from his patients' skin, focusing on the life force energy in different parts of the individual's body—head, feet, stomach, and so on. While Usui was not a scientist, those who came for Reiki treatment did attest to its stress relieving and healing abilities. And so, the practice grew in popularity and gained practitioners across the world. In 2006 alone, 1.2 million adult Americans paid for a Reiki session to help them deal with health issues including depression, anxiety, and chronic pain (Barnes et al., 2007).

Although the energy healing properties of Reiki are immensely beneficial, it should not be used as a replacement for orthodox treatments. However, it complements and enhances the results of standard medicine.

Reiki practitioners are not faith healers, and would not profess to be the cause of the healing that takes place after a successful session. Think of them as conduits for positive energy. Through years of training, such people master the ability to channel that energy through themselves into their patients' bodies. This enhances the positive flow of energy in the recipient's body.

Energy healing can help to improve sleep, reduce anxiety, and give the patient more control over their emotions.

If you have decided to attend an energy healing session, the question then becomes which Reiki master to go to. Since one of Archangel Michael's abilities is to heal, he can guide you to the practitioner that is best suited for you. Saint Michael has watched over and loved you from the day you came into existence, and, hard as it might be to believe, he knows you better than you could ever know yourself. In leading you to the Reiki practitioner that you need, he will consider things like your history, personality, finances, phobias, and values. He will also protect you by making sure you go to trustworthy and right-thinking individuals. If you are yet to write Michael a letter or are planning to write another, you can ask for his guidance as a part of your request.

Since Reiki is about channeling positive energy, unblocking your *ki*, and living a more rewarding life, it often involves a lot of meditation. No, you do not have to be an expert to effectively meditate. It is also not always necessary to remain in a single spot. All that is important is the right atmosphere and singularity of thought. For this reason, consider getting as much Reiki music as you can find. They are everywhere and often downloadable for free. It is as easy as opening your YouTube app and typing *"Reiki songs."* If you went for a session, your Reiki master will play such songs to make sure you are relaxed as good energy sweeps through you. In the midst of such calming and cleansing songs is the best time to receive from Saint Michael. The songs are typically devoid of words, and only contain the healing instrumentals. Let them play while you sit, lie down, or go about your daily house chores. However, you do have to desire the healing and cleansing energy that is activated by the Reiki. Do not resist or forget it. You should remain willing and accepting in both your mind and soul. Whether you are cleaning or writing a book, make sure to not speak. This is because, while Reiki songs are powerful, your attention to them will further guarantee their effectiveness. Also, drinking water after a Reiki session aids your energy healing. By doing all these, your connection with Michael is strengthened, and he will bless all your benevolent wishes.

DAILY LIFE WITH ARCHANGEL MICHAEL

Although Saint Michael is unarguably superior to human beings, he does not behave like a boss, lecturer, dictator, or an uptight parent. The relationships formed with Michael or any other angel are usually the happiest and most fulfilling. We are, in fact, incapable of forming such a bond with any other human being or animal. Archangel Michael is kind and humble, and seeks to teach us how to live our lives in the same way. As you interact with other people in your life, ask Michael to teach you the best way to treat them. You might be a parent, manager, employee, or entrepreneur. Michael can teach you how to always arrive at win-win scenarios, and the right way to get people to do things without being manipulative.

Your romantic life should not be exempt from Michael's counsel. If you find yourself in constant disagreements with your partner, ask him for guidance. You need to know which battles to fight with your romantic partner and how exactly to fight them. No such relationship can last for years without some arguments, but Michael can teach you to approach them with love, kindness, and respect. Graciously, the archangel is also willing to teach you about forgiveness. Some relationships are worth sticking out. However, it might be impossible to do so if you cannot move past hurt feelings and certain betrayals. If you ask for his help, Saint Michael will bless you with the courage to forgive the missteps of your loved ones, and he will also heal the broken relationship.

You also need angelic wisdom to know when a romantic partnership is no longer healthy to continue. To remain in such toxicity is to invite the lower energies of anger, depression, fatigue, and anxiety into your life. But, human discernment in such issues is quite unreliable. Your decision could be marred by your lack of foresight, your growing sexual interest for another person, and other biases. To ensure that you make the right choices, you must depend on the judgement of Archangel Michael.

Were you cleaning the kitchen sink and it suddenly became clogged, and you are now at a loss for how to fix the problem? Before reaching for your phone to use Google, call on Michael first. Even though it seems like a silly thing, Archangel Michael wants to be involved and wants to be included in every area of your life. Let him instruct you on how to fix the clogged sink, or guide you to the right online information. You must understand that you will never be a bother for Saint Michael. If your car battery dies on your way to work and you are about to spiral into self-hate and anxiety, put on some Reiki music and say a quick prayer to the archangel. Accept his divine wisdom, peace, and humor into your soul. Soon, you will be relaxed, happy, and gain understanding on how to deal with that issue.

It is good that you respect and revere Archangel Michael. But he wants to be your friend—and friends share everything with each other, don't they? He wants to cradle you in his wings when you are sad, laugh with you in life's funny moments, and celebrate with your joy. He is an archangel that wants to be with you at your most human times. You have everything to gain by accepting him.

AFTERWORD

Every journey begins with a desire, but it will require determination and courage to complete it: two virtues that you have proven to have by getting to this part of the book. Please, do not stop here. Let your walk with the archangel continue to flourish long after reading. Be reassured by the fact that Michael's love, light, and strength will always be with you.

Hopefully, you have resolved to let the archangel into every aspect of your life. Whether you need help with training or treating your pet, fixing home appliances, applying for a job, or handling your spouse's emotions, Michael is by your side to help you. Write him a letter and focus your energy for the manifestation of your desires, as you have learned from this book. Also, be attuned to the various ways by which he might reply to you. Take water after a Reiki session and try to sleep early. Take care of yourself. You can come back to this book whenever you need to, and as often as you need to. Best wishes on your journey with Michael.

REFERENCES

Barnes, P. M., Bloom, B., & Nahin, R. L. (2008). Complementary and alternative medicine use among adults and children: United States, 2007. *National health statistics reports*, (12), 1–23. https://pubmed.ncbi.nlm.nih.gov/19361005/

Bedosky, L. (2020, May 13). *All about Reiki: how this type of energy healing works, and its health benefits.* Everyday Health. https://www.everydayhealth.com/reiki/

Camp, L. (2018, March 29). From archangel Michael: karma. Lacey Camp. https://www.google.com/amp/s/www.laceycamp.com/single-post/2018/03/29/From-ArchAngel-Michael-Karma%3f_amp_

Gray, K. (2015, February 10). *How to connect with your guardian angel through writing.* Heal Your Life. https://www.healyourlife.com/how-to-connect-with-your-guardian-angel-through-writing

Hopler, W. (2019, January 15). *How to recognize archangel Raphael.* Learn Religions. https://www.learnreligions.com/how-to-recognize-archangel-raphael-124281

Hopler, W. (2019, March 18). *Meet archangel Michael, leader of all the angels.* Learn Religions. https://www.learnreligions.com/meet-archangel-michael-leader-of-angels-124715

Hopler, W. (2019, April 29). *How to recognize archangel Gabriel.* Learn Religions. https://www.learnreligions.com/how-to-recognize-archangel-gabriel-124274

House, A., & Pichereau. C. (n.d.). *How Reiki works with the chakra system.* Dummies. https://www.dummies.com/religion/spirituality/how-reiki-works-with-the-chakra-system/

How to tell when St. Michael is watching over you. (2017, April 25). Original Botanica. https://www.originalbotanica.com/blog/st-michael-watching-over-with-you/

Newman, T. (2017, September 6). *Everything you need to know about Reiki.* Medical News Today. https://www.medicalnewstoday.com/articles/308772

Originals, M. (2012, June 22). *Archangel Michael.* Medium. https://medium.com/mysticaltalk/archangel-michael-7897ad931ae3

Patel, K. (n.d.). *Reiki healing for beginners.* Goop. https://goop.com/wellness/spirituality/reiki-for-beginners

Patel, R. (2018, July 10). *Working with archangel Uriel.* Reiki Rays. https://reikirays.com/42828/working-with-archangel-uriel/

Redd, N., T. (2019, February 7). *How old is the earth?* Space. https://www.space.com/24854-how-old-is-earth.html

Saint Michael archangel. (2015, November 17). Curious Curandera. http://curiouscurandera.blogspot.com/2015/11/saint-michael-archangel.html?m=1

St. Michael amparo for protection. (n.d.). Creole Moon. https://www.creolemoon.com/store/p677/St._Michael_Amparo_for_Protection.html#

Virtue, D. (n.d.). *8 ways to recognize archangel Michael.* Belief Net. https://www.beliefnet.com/inspiration/angels/2008/12/8-ways-to-recognize-archangel-michael.aspx

YOUR FEEDBACK IS VALUED

From the bottom of my heart, thank you for reading my book. I truly hope that it helps you on your spiritual journey and to live a more empowered and happy life. If it does help you, then I'd like to ask you for a favor. Would you be kind enough to leave an honest review for this book on Amazon? It'd be greatly appreciated and will likely impact the lives of other spiritual seekers across the globe, giving them hope and power.

Thank you and good luck,

Angela Grace

Why not join our Facebook community and discuss your spiritual path with like-minded seekers?

We would love to hear from you!

Go here to join the 'Ascending Vibrations' community: bit.ly/ascendingvibrations

Printed in Great Britain
by Amazon

84767456R00034